EARLY LEARNING
For three- to five-year-old

Dad's Day

Story by Pie Corbett
Activities by David Bell, Pie Corbett
Geoff Leyland and Mick Seller

Illustrations by Diann Timms

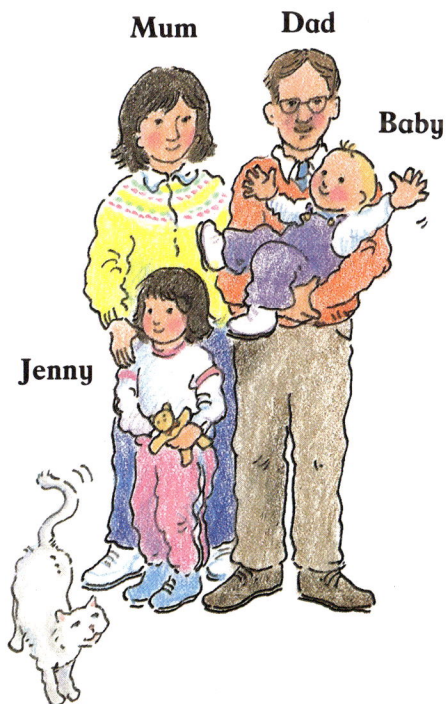

Mum Dad Baby

Jenny

For Caroline

Mum and Jenny and Baby
were up and dressed.

They'd had breakfast.

What do you like for breakfast?
Ask everyone in your family what
their favourite breakfast would be.
Do you all agree?

After a good breakfast, what would
be a really good day for you?
What would be a really terrible day?

Start a scrapbook of drawings or
postcards from days out you
have enjoyed.

'Hurry up, or we'll be late,' shouted Mum.

Dad was still in bed.

What sorts of things does your mum often say?

What about your dad? Does he have any favourite sayings?

Do you know any old people who have favourite sayings?

Jenny and Baby woke Dad up.

I wonder what Dad was dreaming about.

Do you have dreams? What sorts of funny things happen in your dreams?

What sorts of stories do you like to have read to you before you go to sleep? Which is your favourite story?

They were going to the zoo.

Point to the wheels of the car.
How many can you see?
Does the car have any other wheels
that you can think of?

Point to and count the doors on the car.
How many doors are open?
How many doors are closed?

It wasn't Dad's day.

He fed buns to the elephants and got told off...

PLEASE DO NOT FEED THE ANIMALS

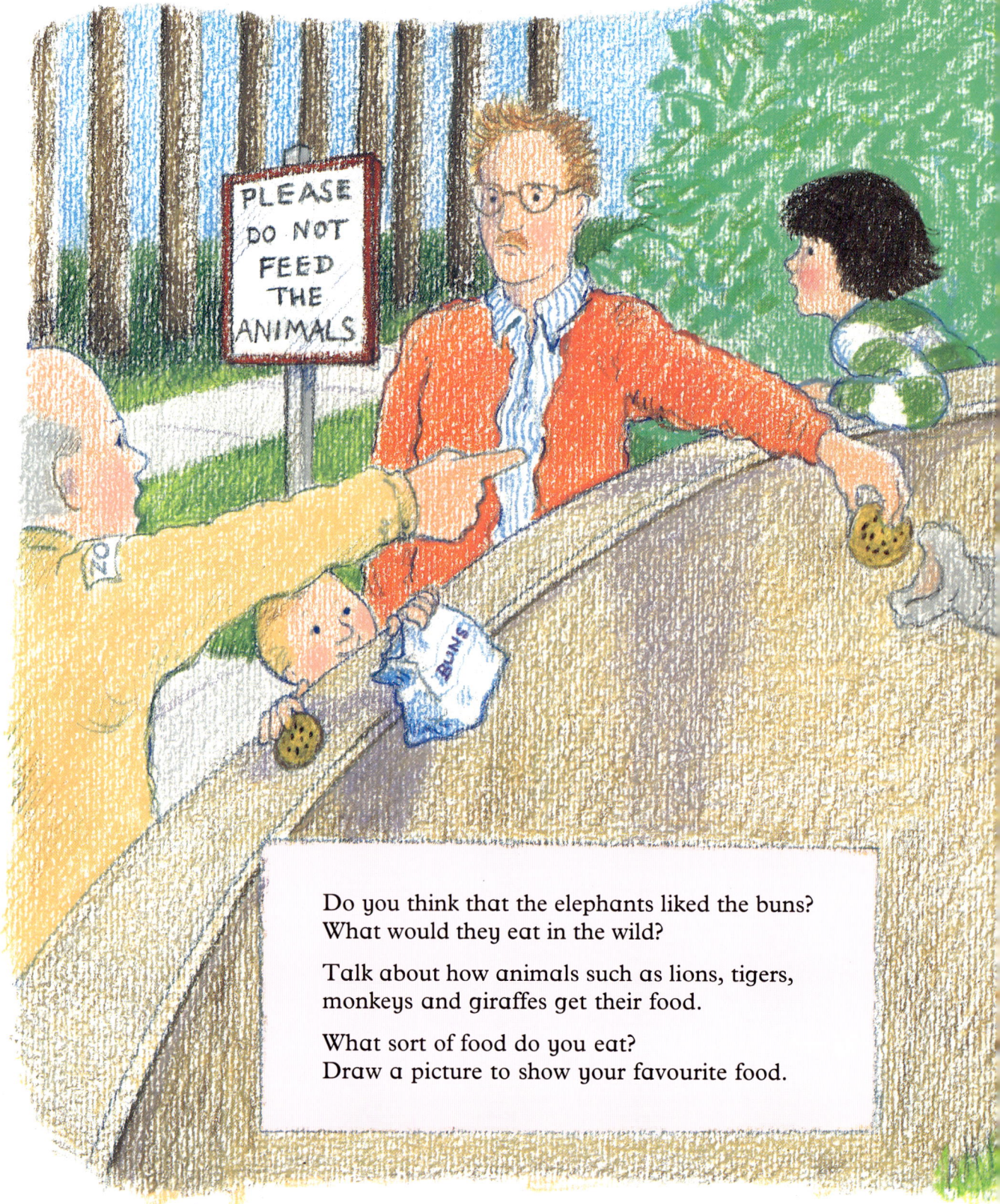

Do you think that the elephants liked the buns?
What would they eat in the wild?

Talk about how animals such as lions, tigers,
monkeys and giraffes get their food.

What sort of food do you eat?
Draw a picture to show your favourite food.

...tripped over his laces...

The shoe laces are in a criss-cross pattern.
If a lace was taken out of a shoe, could you
put it back in a criss-cross pattern?
You might need someone to help get
you started.

Can you draw a criss-cross pattern on a
piece of paper? Try to copy the pattern you
see in the picture.

...dropped his ice-cream...

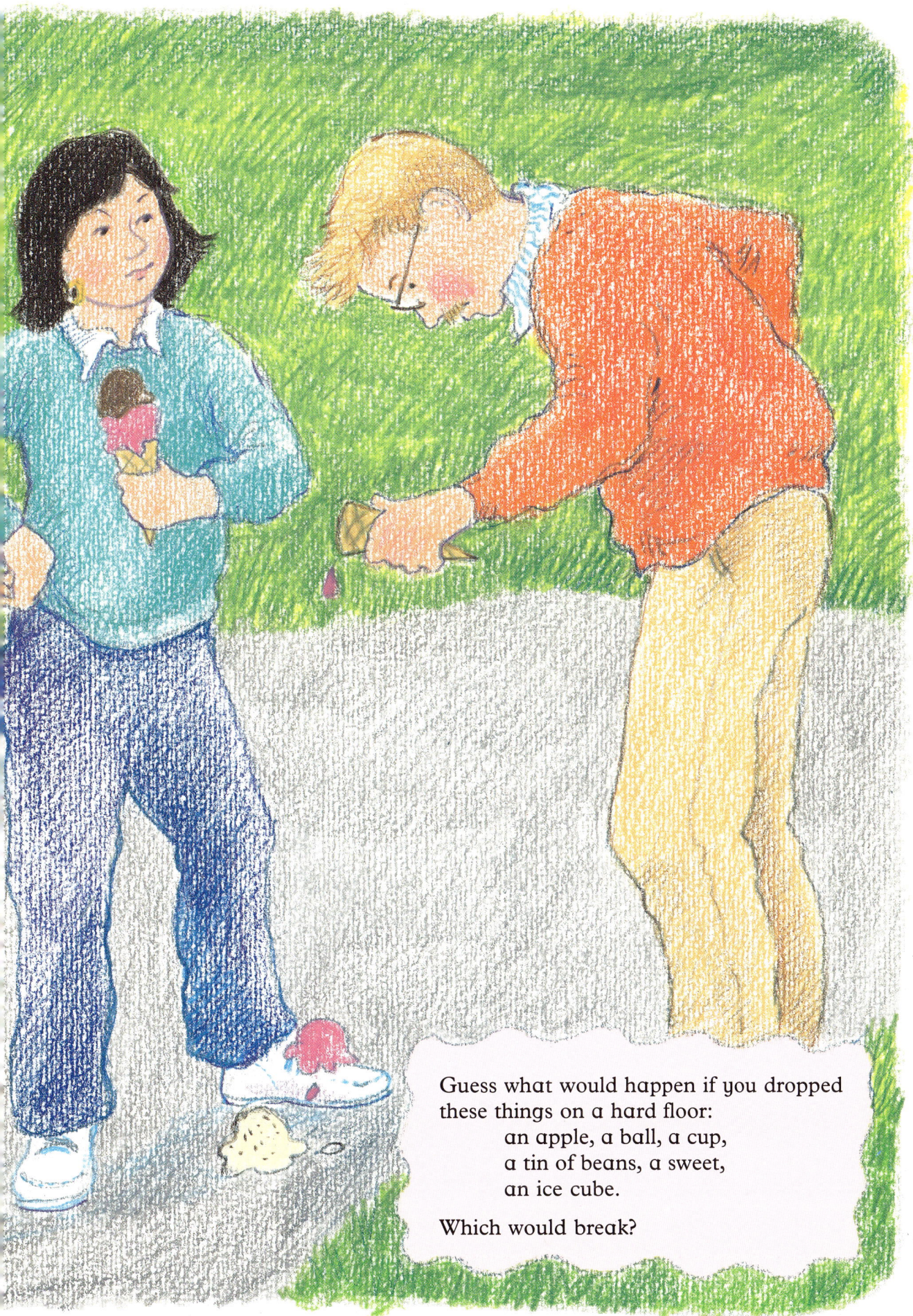

Guess what would happen if you dropped
these things on a hard floor:
      an apple, a ball, a cup,
      a tin of beans, a sweet,
      an ice cube.

Which would break?

...let a camel eat the picnic...

How many humps has the camel?
How many humps do two camels have?
Try drawing three camels like the
ones in the picture.
How many humps would three camels
have altogether?

...got told off by a parrot...

Have you ever heard a parrot talking?

What sorts of things do parrots say?
Are they really talking?
Can you understand what
they're saying?

Try drawing your favourite animal.

...was growled at by the lions...

The lions look fierce. Can you make a fierce face?

When you look at somebody's face, you can usually tell how they're feeling.

Here's a feeling game to play with someone.
Take it in turns to pull one of these faces:
        happy, cross, tired, sad.
The other person has to guess which face you are pulling.
You could make up some more faces yourself.

...made faces with the monkeys...

Which monkey is the biggest?
Which monkey is the smallest?
Which monkey is the fattest?
Which monkey is the thinnest?

Face someone and ask them to copy the movements you make with your arms and legs. Then change over so that you are doing the copying.

...and when he nearly fell
in the snake pit,
Mum was really mad.

The letter 'S' looks rather like a snake.

Could you draw a row of snakes?
Start the letter at the top and draw downwards.

You could colour your snakes and give them faces.

Look out for the letter 'S' on signs and packets.

They drove home in silence.

When you're in the car, talk about how many things you can see that make a sound.

Draw some pictures of noisy cars.

When they arrived home, Dad put his hand in his pocket for the key.

Oh no! It wasn't there!

How can you tell what's in your pocket before you put your hand in?

Ask someone to put some different things into their coat pocket without showing you what they are. Try to guess what they are by feeling the shapes through the pocket.

Lucky for Dad, Mum had a spare.

Baby, Mum and Jenny gave Dad a big cuddle to make him feel better.

Who is standing behind Dad?

Is there anyone beside him?
Is there anyone in front of him?

Mum has found the key.
Where will it go?

Activity Notes

Pages 2-3 Keeping a scrapbook of special days and holidays is a good way to encourage a sense of purpose for children's drawing and writing - especially if the books are shown to grandparents or friends. Write down what your child wants to say and let them draw pictures to show what happened.

Pages 4-5 Very young children soon pick up favourite sayings. This activity is an enjoyable way to consider how people use language. Listen for different sayings and explain what they mean. Tape-recording friends and family members with different accents can be fun. It is important that children enjoy and appreciate other accents and do not think they are inferior to their own.

Pages 6-7 If possible, take your child to the library every week and let them choose some books alone. Learning to make sensible choices and having favourite authors and illustrators is part of becoming a reader. Probably the single most important thing a parent can do for their child educationally, is to read stories every day, and make the story session *enjoyable*.

Pages 8-9 Opportunities for maths are all around and young children should be encouraged to find things to count wherever they can. Simple numbers such as threes, fours and fives are best dealt with at this stage, and there are plenty of starting points around the home.

Pages 10-11 When discussing the types of food which animals eat, introduce the idea of grouping them, initially into two groups: meat eaters and plant eaters.
After this, you may be able to support the ideas by painting pictures of animals eating what you think might be their favourite food!

Pages 12-13 Copying patterns assists children's understanding of detail and shape, as well as developing hand-eye co-ordination. Shoe treads make patterns; compare different treads and talk about significant similarities and differences.

Pages 14-15 Follow the first guesses about whether objects would break with questions which encourage thought about what objects are made from, eg 'Will it bounce?', 'Why?', 'What's it made from?'.
Collect six objects which can be safely dropped. Ask your child to predict what will happen when each is dropped. Test their ideas. Talk again about what materials the objects are made from.

Pages 16-17 Making groups of objects in twos, threes or fours helps counting skills, but it also lays the foundation for later work in multiplication. Encourage children to find natural groups of objects, eg two hands, or to make their own groups, eg three building bricks.

Pages 18-19 This activity makes the distinction between imitation and talking. Talk has meaning, imitation may not. It is fun, for example, to try to speak like a parrot. Drawing favourites is important and so, too, is talking about *why* you like something.

Pages 20-21 People, like animals, have a range of ways of communicating and showing their feelings. These may involve body movements, noises and facial expressions.
Develop the game by drawing some pictures to show happy faces and sad faces. Try drawing a sleepy or an angry face. Discuss others you may be able to draw or paint.

Pages 22-23 Children use the language of measurement in a very imprecise way and they often confuse the terms. At this stage it is helpful to keep together appropriate comparisons such as biggest-smallest, fattest-thinnest or tallest-shortest.

Pages 24-25 Letter shapes can be introduced enjoyably, but you should ensure that the shapes are correctly formed. Show your child how to write their name using capital letters to start and then continuing in small letters.

Pages 26-27 This activity encourages observation and thought about the source and variety of sounds. Develop this idea by collecting pictures of other things that make a noise and then making a 'noisy' picture.

Pages 28-29 When your child guesses, ask 'Why do you think it's a ...?'. In this way, you can build up their skills of predicting after considering the evidence, eg, 'I think it's a ... because of its shape and the sound it makes when I shake it.'.
Make a collection of familiar objects such as toys. With their eyes closed, ask your child whether they can identify each object while wearing a pair of mittens or gloves.

Pages 30-31 Positional language needs to be developed if children are to have an understanding of shape and space. Simple words like 'beside', 'behind', 'above', etc, can be used in day-to-day conversation and as your child is asked to perform simple tasks, eg 'Put your shoes under the bed.'.